S0-ARI-491

Joseph

Massachusetts

32716

DATE DUE

JUL 20, 2017	

PRINTED IN U.S.A.

The United States

Massachusetts

Paul Joseph
ABDO & Daughters

visit us at
www.abdopub.com

Published by Abdo & Daughters, 4940 Viking Drive, Suite 622, Edina, Minnesota 55435.
Copyright © 1998 by Abdo Consulting Group, Inc., Pentagon Tower, P.O. Box 36036, Minne-apolis, Minnesota 55435 USA. International copyrights reserved in all countries. No part of this book may be reproduced in any form without written permission from the publisher.

Printed in the United States.

Cover and Interior Photo credits: SuperStock, Peter Arnold, Inc., Corbis-Bettmann, Wide World
Edited by Lori Kinstad Pupeza
Contributing editor Brooke Henderson
Special thanks to our Checkerboard Kids—Morgan Roberts, Raymond Sherman, Priscilla Cáceres

All statistics taken from the 1990 census; The Rand McNally Discovery Atlas of The United States. Other sources: Compton's Encyclopedia, 1997; *Masssachusetts*, Children's Press, Chicago, 1989.

Library of Congress Cataloging-in-Publication Data

Joseph, Paul, 1970-
       Massachusetts / by Paul Joseph.
       p.   cm. -- (United States)
       Includes index.
       Summary: Surveys the people, geograph, and history of the northeastern state known as the "Bay State."
       ISBN 1-56239-882-2
       1. Massachusetts--Juvenile literature. {1. Massachusetts.} I. Title. II. Series: United States (Series).
       F64.3.J67   1998
       974.4--dc21   97-18132
                                                           CIP
                                                           AC

Contents

Welcome to Massachusetts

The state of Massachusetts is located in the northeast part of the United States. It is one of the New England states. Massachusetts is bordered on the north by New Hampshire and Vermont. New York is on the west. Connecticut and Rhode Island are to the south. The Atlantic Ocean borders the entire east coast of Massachusetts.

The name Massachusetts comes from Algonquian words that mean "near the great mountain." Many think the **Native Americans** were talking about the Blue Hills in the state. Massachusetts is also called the Bay State. That is a nickname people gave it because the first settlements were on Cape Cod Bay.

The beautiful state of Massachusetts is filled with thick forests, rocky beaches on the coast, and tall mountains.

No other state has as much American history as Massachusetts. The Mayflower landed at Plymouth, Massachusetts, in December of 1620. From that point on, the United States as we know it began to take shape.

Massachusetts continued to pave the way throughout American history. Harvard was the first American college. The first regular newspaper was published in the state. The first shots of the **American Revolution** were fired in Massachusetts, which later gave the United States independence from England.

Martha's Vineyard, Massachusetts.

Fast Facts

MASSACHUSETTS

Capital and largest city
Boston (574,283 people)

Area
7,826 square miles
(20,269 sq km)

Population
6,029,051 people
Rank: 13th

Statehood
Feb. 6, 1788
(6th state admitted)

Principal river
Connecticut River

Highest point
Mount Greylock;
3,491 feet (1,064 m)

Motto
Ense petit placidam sub libertate quietem (By the sword we seek peace, but peace only under liberty)

Song
"All Hail to Massachusetts"

Famous People
John Adams, John Quincy Adams, Louisa May Alcott, Leonard Bernstein, Emily Dickinson, Ralph Waldo Emerson, John F. Kennedy

Massachusetts is one of the original 13 colonies

13

*S*tate Flag

*M*ayflower

*C*hickadee

*E*lm

About Massachusetts
The Bay State

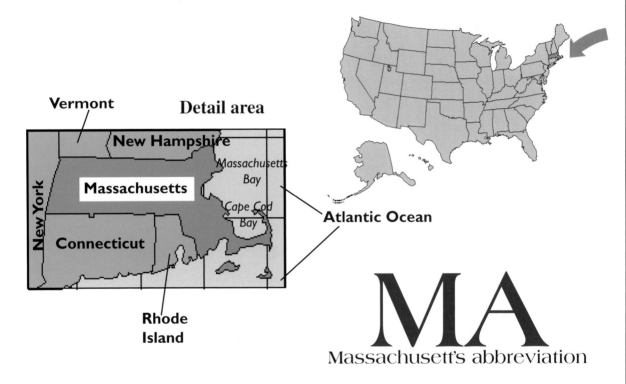

Vermont

Detail area

New Hampshire

Massachusetts Bay

New York

Massachusetts

Cape Cod Bay

Atlantic Ocean

Connecticut

Rhode Island

MA
Massachusett's abbreviation

Borders: west (New York), north (Vermont, New Hampshire), east (Atlantic Ocean), south (Connecticut, Rhode Island)

Nature's Treasures

The waters of the Bay State attract many visitors. The Atlantic Ocean is good for fishing, fun water sports, and sandy beaches.

Land, lakes, and rivers dot the state. Walden Pond was made famous by Henry David Thoreau. He wrote about the pond in his book *Walden*.

The state's forests cover more than three million acres of land. Most of the trees in Massachusetts are birch, beech, maple, oak, white pine, and hemlock. Because forests cover a lot of Massachusetts's land, there are many parks for walking, hiking, and sightseeing.

The climate in Massachusetts is also a treasure. The spring, summer, and fall months have wonderful weather, which makes this northeastern state a delight to visit. The winters are mild on the coast, however, inland it can get very cold.

Sunrise on Walden Pond, Concord, Massachusetts.

Beginnings

Some believe that over 1,000 years ago Vikings landed on Cape Cod. But the first known people to live in Massachusetts were **Native Americans**. The different groups were called the Nauset, the Massachuset, and the Wampanoag.

In 1620, Europeans sailed across the Atlantic Ocean in their Mayflower ship and settled at Plymouth. The **settlers** were a group of about 100 people called Pilgrims. The Pilgrims broke away from the Church of England and came to America so they could choose their own religion.

The Pilgrims set up places to live, practiced their own religion, and made peace with the Native Americans. They even celebrated the first Thanksgiving with the Native Americans.

Soon, other Europeans began coming across the ocean to America. Many were from England and were known as

Puritans. The Puritans found Boston and other settlements. Puritan John Winthrop became the first **governor** of the colony, around 1630.

Massachusetts was under the control of England. Many people didn't like this. England was making these citizens pay a lot of added money for goods—this is known as a tax. The people of Massachusetts revolted and stopped buying English goods. In 1773, Samuel Adams inspired the Boston Tea Party, where people dumped British tea into the Boston Harbor to protest the tea tax.

Wars began breaking out in the state between England and America. In 1776, America declared its independence from England and the **American Revolution** began. After America defeated England in the war, the United States began to form. Massachusetts became the sixth state on February 6, 1788.

A replica of the Mayflower.

B.C. to 1636

Early Land and Settlers

 The first known people to occupy what is now Massachusetts were **Native Americans**.

 1620: Pilgrims land in Massachusetts.

 1621: The Pilgrims and the Native Americans celebrate the first Thanksgiving in Plymouth.

 1632: Boston is made the capital of the Massachusetts Bay Colony.

 1636: The first college in the United States, Harvard University, is opened.

Massachusetts

B.C. to 1636

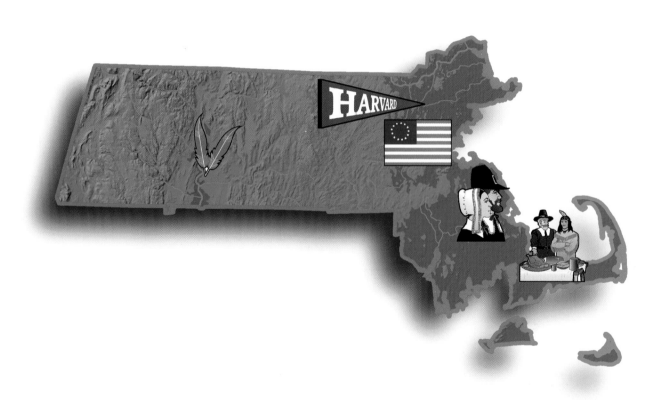

13

1773 to 1897

Independence to Statehood

 1773: The people of Boston protest England's taxes by dumping England's tea into the bay. This is known as the Boston Tea Party.

 1776: America declares its independence from England. The start of the **American Revolution** begins in Massachusetts.

 1788: Massachusetts becomes the sixth state on February 6.

 1796: John Adams, of Quincy, Massachusetts, is elected second president of the United States.

 1824: John Q. Adams, son of John Adams, is elected sixth president of the United States.

 1897: Boston completes the first subway in the United States.

14

Massachusetts

1773 to 1897

1923 to Present

Massachusetts in the 1900s

 1923: Calvin Coolidge, of Northampton, Massachusetts, is elected 30th president of the United States.

 1960: John F. Kennedy of Brookline, Massachusetts, is elected 35th president of the United States.

 1966: Edward W. Brooke, of Massachusetts, is the first African American in history to be elected to the United States **Senate**.

 1986: The Boston Celtics win their record 16th NBA Championship.

16

Massachusetts

1923 to Present

BALLOT

Pittsfield

Worcester, Framingham

Lynn
Malden
Somerville
Waltham
Cambridge
Brookline
Boston
Quincy
Weymouth

Chicopee

Springfield

Brockton

New
Bedford

Massachusetts's People

There are just over six million people living in the state of Massachusetts. It is the 13th most populated state in the country. The first known people to live in the state were **Native Americans**.

There are many well known people who have come from Massachusetts. The most well known from the state is a family—the Kennedys. Father Joe Kennedy was a wealthy businessman who later was **ambassador** to England. His wife, Rose Fitzgerald Kennedy, came from a well known Boston family.

John F. Kennedy, their son, was 35th president of the United States. He was the second youngest president at 43. He graduated from Harvard college and later was a U.S. **representative** and **senator** from Massachusetts. This handsome and smart president was **assassinated** in Dallas in 1963.

Other Kennedy sons Robert and Edward also were involved in politics. Robert was a senator, U.S. Attorney General, and ran for president before he too, was shot and killed. Edward has been the U.S. senator of Massachusetts since 1962.

Massachusetts is also known for its world famous writers and poets. They include Ralph Waldo Emerson, Nathaniel Hawthorne, Henry David Thoreau, Robert Frost, Louisa May Alcott, and Phillis Wheatley, the first African American woman poet.

Henry David Thoreau

Phillis Wheatley

John F. Kennedy

Historic Cities

Massachusetts has many splendid cities in its state. Most people from the state live in cities. More than four out of every five people in Massachusetts live in cities and towns. The rest live in **rural** areas.

Boston is the state capital and largest city in Massachusetts. It is known for its American history. Many tourists visit this city for its historic sites.

Boston is one of the chief seaports on the Atlantic Ocean. It has many **fisheries**. Boston is also known as a great sportstown. The Celtics NBA basketball team is one of the most famous teams in all of sports. The Red Sox in baseball and the Bruins in hockey are also in Boston.

Worcester, the second largest city in Massachusetts, is in the middle of the state. It is

Cambridge

Boston

Springfield

Worcester

New Bedford

known as an **industrial** town. It also is home to museums, festivals, Clark University, and the University of Massachusetts Medical School.

Cambridge is an historic city. It is located on the Charles River and is known for its colleges. Harvard University is the oldest and most famous college in the United States. Other excellent colleges in Cambridge include Radcliffe College and Massachusetts Institute of Technology (MIT).

Other splendid cities in Massachusetts include Springfield, New Bedford, Newton, Wellesley, Lowell, and Lynn, among others.

Boats moored at pier in Gloucester, Massachusetts.

Massachusetts's Land

Massachusetts has some of the most beautiful land in the country. There are sandy beaches, forests, lakes, and rivers spread out across the state. The state is divided into four distinct regions.

The Coastal Plain region covers the most eastern part of the state. This area is shaped like an arm flexing its muscle. It is a sandy area that includes Cape Cod, fishing villages, and many wonderful summer resorts.

The Seaboard Lowland region stretches across the entire eastern part of Massachusetts except for the arm. On the coast it covers the entire Massachusetts Bay. Inland, the region has many rivers and hills.

The New England Upland region covers the central part of Massachusetts. It has many streams and rivers. The largest river in this region is the Connecticut River. The area is also dotted with hills.

The Berkshire Hills region covers the western part of the state. There are three ranges of mountains in this region. In the far west is the Taconic Mountains. In the east are the Berkshire Hills. And in the north is the Hoosac Range.

This mostly forested region has many rivers running through it. Mount Greylock, in the northwest part of the region, is the highest point in the state at 3,491 feet (1,064 m).

The Cape Cod seashore

Massachusetts at Play

Massachusetts is a great place to play. It is a very popular state for tourists. People are attracted to the sandy beaches on the east coast and the wooded hills of the western part of the state.

People enjoy the beautiful summers at seaside resorts on Cape Cod, Cape Ann, and the nearby islands. At these resorts people can swim, boat, fish, and sail.

In western Massachusetts, the Berkshire Hills area has mountains, clear lakes, thick forests, and beautiful resorts. People enjoy hiking, biking, camping, fishing, skiing, and sightseeing there.

Many visitors enjoy the rich history of Massachusetts. Throughout the state, and especially in Boston, people can see American history before their eyes in buildings, monuments, museums, and libraries.

Massachusetts's warm summers are fun on the coast.

Massachusetts at Work

The people of Massachusetts must work to make money. There are many different kinds of jobs that people do in the state. With the tourists that visit the state each year, a lot of people work in service jobs. Service is working in hotels, resorts, restaurants, and stores.

Many people in Massachusetts work in the **manufacturing industry**. Some people make electronic equipment, others print or publish books or magazines, while others make paper. There are many other manufacturing jobs in the state too.

Because Massachusetts lies on the Atlantic Ocean, many people from the state work in **fisheries**. Some of the fish caught and sold in the state are haddock, flounder, cod, whiting, and ocean perch. People working in fisheries, however, try to catch lobsters, clams, and sea scallops because they are worth the most money. A lot of the fish you eat comes from these **fisheries**.

There are many different things to do and see in the great state of Massachusetts. Because of its natural beauty, the people, coast, resorts, and history, the Bay State is a great place to visit, live, work, and play.

Many people in Massachusetts work in the fishing industry.

Fun Facts

•On the night of April 18, 1775, Paul Revere rode through Massachusetts shouting, "The British are coming!" Revere, one of the leaders of the Boston Tea Party in 1773, warned the people in Concord and Lexington in just enough time. Because of Revere, they were ready to fight the British army, who arrived the next morning.

•Cape Cod is a very beautiful and well known **peninsula** in Massachusetts. Its land thrusts into the Atlantic Ocean like a giant arm bent at the elbow.

•Boston became the capital in 1632. At that time, the area was known as the Massachusetts Bay Colony. Today, Boston continues to be the capital of the state and one of the most famous cities in the world.

•Four presidents of the United States were from the state of Massachusetts. John Adams was the second president of the United States. His son, John Q. Adams, was the sixth president. Calvin Coolidge, who was **governor** of Massachusetts, was the 30th president. John F. Kennedy, who was a **senator** in Massachusetts, was the 35th president.

This statue is in honor of Paul Revere.

Glossary

Ambassador: a person who works for their country in another country.

American Revolution: a war that gave the United States its independence from Great Britain.

Assassinated: the murder of a very important person.

Fisheries: the business of catching fish.

Governor: the highest elected official in the state.

Industrial: big businesses such as factories or manufacturing.

Industry: many different types of businesses.

Manufacture: to make things by machine in a factory.

Native Americans: the first people who were born in and occupied North America.

Peninsula: a long narrow piece of land that extends into the water.

Representative: a person that is elected by the people to represent a certain area.

Rural: outside of the city.

Senate: Also known as congress, is a group of 100 elected senators (two from each state) that represent their state and make laws for the country.

Senator: one of two elected officials from a state that represents the state in Washington D.C. There they make laws and are part of Congress.

Settlers: people that move to a new land where no one has lived before and build a community, or settlement.

Internet Sites

A Perfect Day in Boston
http://www.bostbest.com/
The most exciting part of any trip away from home is the discovery of those "special places" that represent the character, talent, and culture of a particular city. It is our pleasure to offer you some unique and wonderful spots that represent the Best in Boston, places you will never find in other cities of America.

Beantown Basics
http://staff.motiv.co.uk/~carnold/boston/
Boston, home of the cod, the Red Sox, the Bruins, the Lowells and the Cabots, Leonard Nimoy, Juliana Hatfield, the Celtics, that large Citgo sign, The Hancock Building, The Prudential Building, and the Charles River, is a jewel. It has been called the Athens of America and the Hub of the Universe.

Cape Cod
http://www.capecod.com/index.html
Online details on Cape Cod shopping, lodging, attractions and dining. Also featured here are Cape Cod maps and town information, a monthly calendar of events for JULY & AUGUST and Kids Calendar.

These sites are subject to change. Go to your favorite search engine and type Massachusetts for more information.

PASS IT ON

Tell Others Something Special About Your State

To educate readers around the country, pass on interesting tips, places to see, history, and little unknown facts about the state you live in. We want to hear from you!

To get posted on ABDO & Daughters website E-mail us at "mystate@abdopub.com"

Index